D1551005

GERMÁN

GARMENDIA

STAR CHILEAN GAMER WITH 10 BILLION+ VIEWS

Kevin Hall

rosen publishing's
rosen
central®

New York

Published in 2020 by The Rosen Publishing Group, Inc.
29 East 21st Street, New York, NY 10010

Library of Congress Cataloging-in-Publication Data

Names: Hall, Kevin, 1990– author.
Title: Germán Garmendia: Star Chilean Gamer with 10 Billion+ Views / Kevin Hall.
Description: First edition. | New York : Rosen Central, 2020. | Series: Top
video gamers in the world | Includes bibliographical references and index.
Identifiers: LCCN 2018048739| ISBN 9781725346079
(library bound) | ISBN 9781725346062 (pbk.)
Subjects: LCSH: Garmendia, Germán, 1990– —Juvenile literature.
| Internet personalities—Chile—Biography—Juvenile literature. |
YouTube (Electronic resource)—Biography—Juvenile literature.
Classification: LCC PN1992.9236.G68 H36 2019 | DDC 792.7/6028092 [B]—dc23
LC record available at https://lccn.loc.gov/2018048739

Manufactured in the United States of America

On the cover: Shown here at the 2014 MTV Millennial Awards, Germán
Garmendia has turned his successful YouTube videos into a multimedia career.

CONTENTS

What makes a YouTube star? YouTube is home to many celebrities who upload videos every day, gaining millions of subscribers along the way. There are thousands of categories that YouTube users can browse to watch videos and creators that interest them. Whether a user is interested in sports, cooking, movies, books, pop culture, or anything else, there are YouTube videos and channels tailored to their specific interests.

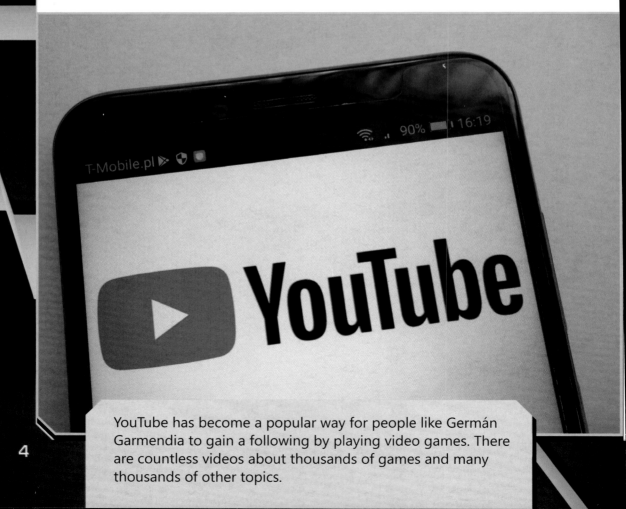

YouTube has become a popular way for people like Germán Garmendia to gain a following by playing video games. There are countless videos about thousands of games and many thousands of other topics.

Beginning in the early 2000s and truly expanding in the 2010s, YouTube features many online stars who have created channels that have made a huge impact on the online community. These creators acquire millions of subscribers who hang on their every word. There is a market for every interest one can think of on YouTube. One of the most significant areas of interest that has exploded in popularity—beginning in the 2010s—is video games. Several YouTube stars have acquired this kind of fame and entertain millions of followers with the content they produce on YouTube. One of these stars is international sensation Germán Garmendia.

To his beloved fans, Garmendia is known for his two YouTube channels: HolaSoyGerman and JuegaGerman. But how did Germán Garmendia rise to fame? How did this YouTube star become so popular, boasting two of the most subscribed channels on YouTube while raking in massive profits? Garmendia's rise to fame is fascinating and speaks to how any content creator—with hard work and vision—can use YouTube to launch his or her own career.

CHAPTER 1

Growing Up Germán

Germán Garmendia was born in Copiapó, Chile, on April 25, 1990. He and his brother, Diego, were raised by his mother for most of their childhood, since his father passed away in a car accident when Germán was only three years old. Before starting his first channel, one of Germán's main passions was music. When he was a teenager, he formed a band called Zudex with his brother. It was not until Germán turned twenty-one that he would first be introduced to the world of YouTube.

Copiapó, Chile, where Garmendia grew up, is a breathtaking place. It is here that his love of video games and making people laugh took shape.

Enter: Germán

In 2011, one of Garmendia's friends encouraged him to start uploading videos to YouTube. His first video was titled "Las cosas obvias de la vida" ("The obvious things in life") and would be the first video uploaded to the channel he would name HolaSoyGerman ("Hello, I'm Germán"). He soon began uploading videos to his channel every week. Slowly but surely, his popularity began to rise. By 2018, HolaSoyGerman became the fifth-most-popular YouTube channel in the world. With HolaSoyGerman alone, he has reached more than thirty million subscribers. What is it about Garmendia and his channel that makes so many people his loyal fans?

Many YouTube stars earn fame by pulling outlandish stunts, creating exaggerated personas, or unfortunately, by buying followers (Garmendia has been accused of this and has denied any wrongdoing). There is not a tried-and-true method that will work for those trying to become famous through their YouTube channels. Some get lucky. Others persist through hard work. However, each case is different; there is no guaranteed formula.

What makes Garmendia's success so interesting is his background. He is a native of Latin America, and nearly all of his videos are in Spanish. How did a Spanish-speaking YouTube star break out, earning so many followers that may or may not speak his native language?

The answer may lie with the target audience for both of Garmendia's channels. He is a little older than most of his viewers (who are in their teenage years), but he is a kid at heart. His videos—both on HolaSoyGerman and his second channel, JuegaGerman—are typically viewed by a younger audience that appreciates his corny jokes and whimsical approach. This is not to say that his channels are only for kids obsessed with video games or plugged into Latin culture, but it certainly does make sense that a huge portion of his subscribers fall into that younger demographic. Young people are by far the most frequent users of YouTube and similar sites, so with content aimed directly at that age range, Garmendia

More and more young people are using YouTube as an entertainment source. No matter what they are interested in, the site has a video for them.

has been set up for success since his first video.

Worthy of Support

Regardless of how influential Spanish-speaking youths have been for his internet career, there is a much simpler reason as to why Garmendia and both of his channels have acquired such success: Germán Garmendia himself. He writes, produces, and edits all the content on his channel. It is not hard to follow and support someone who dedicates himself to a project, and Garmendia and his channels are no exception.

Another thing worth noting is what Garmendia discusses in his channels. He covers topics such as going out to lunch with a friend, applying for jobs, moving, and other parts of everyday life. He is not creating any strange setups that are hard to believe. He is true to life, discussing things about everyday life that his subscribers can relate to and enjoy. He is extremely animated, and none of the jokes involved in his videos are used to attack anyone. He is basically a class clown with a gigantic audience, entertaining his followers (and his friends) with his many videos. The channel HolaSoyGerman, though, has been inactive for a while. However, his second channel, JuegaGerman, remains online and active.

Breaking Out, Branching Out

Latin America's relationship to the internet may also reveal why so many have flocked to Garmendia's channels. Three of the most popular (and most downloaded) apps in Latin American countries are WhatsApp, YouTube, and Facebook. Many kids in these countries log on to YouTube and these other apps every single day.

According to a report by Ben Popper of the Verge, around 80 percent of YouTube's views come from outside the United States. This may account for why stars like Garmendia and others have become so popular. While there is a massive online YouTube community in the United States, YouTube is available to users worldwide. Additionally, many people in the United States are bilingual, and Spanish is the second-most-spoken language. As a result, Garmendia has been able to find a strong fan base even in a mainly English-speaking country.

Like HolaSoyGerman, JuegaGerman has garnered millions upon millions of subscribers.

The End of HolaSoyGerman?

No one truly knows why Garmendia stopped uploading videos to his original channel. It may have been due to the intense workload or the insane commitment to his content. He also had several incidents with fans' behavior.

Despite his past and present success, Garmendia shutting down his original channel speaks to a bigger issue in the YouTube community. Many creators—including Garmendia, PewDiePie, and El Rubius—have announced breaks from producing content online.

Garmendia has focused his attentions solely on his video game content on YouTube. There is no timetable set in place for when, if ever, he will return to his original HolaSoyGerman channel.

They speak of suffering from burnout as the main cause for these breaks. While it may seem that these creators are having the time of their lives producing content online, the reality is much darker.

It can take several hours, days, and even weeks to direct, edit, and upload content to these YouTube channels. This grueling behind-the-scenes aspect of uploading videos is not always obvious to YouTube subscribers. Neither is the mental strain uploading can take. By being open about the negative aspects of content creation, stars like Garmendia and El Rubius have let their subscribers know how being a star on YouTube can take its toll. Whether they intended to or not, these stars have become role models, since they let their followers know that it is okay to not be okay. While creating video game content online may seem like an absolute dream job, these creators can become overwhelmed. Being open about their own feelings lets their subscribers know that it is okay to take time to focus on their own issues, heal, and (hopefully) come back stronger than ever before.

Garmendia has made his mark on the world of YouTube as one of the most famous Spanish-speaking stars the website has ever known—and he did it through comedy and variety videos. After shutting down his original channel, dealing with the stress of constant content creation, and coming back into the public eye, one of his main focuses now is on video games.

JuegaGerman, Gaming Star

Many popular YouTube channels gain subscribers in a very simple way: video games. YouTube Gaming—a sub-website that contains only videos related to video games—has more than seventy million subscribers. These channels offer subscribers various different kinds of content: video game reviews, walkthroughs, tutorials, Let's Plays, and other videos that demonstrate and break down games, such as *Overwatch*, *Fortnite*, *Minecraft*, and countless others.

Fortnite is one of the most successful games of all time, and millions of people tune in every week to watch YouTubers—including Garmendia—play their favorite game.

Video Game Pop Culture

YouTube Gaming's seventy million subscribers are just one indication of how popular video game culture has become. To fill the needs of all these fans, video gamers and video producers (including Garmendia and countless others) have used

YouTube as a platform to reach out, show off their skills, and make gaming a mainstream hobby.

On YouTube, there are seven main forms of video content related to gaming. The first three forms are mainly handled by the companies releasing the games, not people like Garmendia who make videos about them:

- **Announcement:** These videos are typically a few minutes long. They are videos made by the companies producing the games to let players know of an upcoming title.
- **Demonstration (demo):** Similar to an announcement, a demo is a first look at how a game works. These videos are commonly around ten minutes long. Game demos act as introductions for the YouTube gaming community. By limiting gameplay time, demos let potential buyers see if the game they are playing is worth pursuing at all.
- **Launch:** These short videos are simply a reminder to gamers that a game will soon be released to the public. They rarely include new information; instead, they are supposed to excite potential players (and buyers).

There are four other types of videos commonly found on gaming channels. These videos are all produced by people like Garmendia:

- **Game-powered entertainment:** These can take many forms, such as parodies and other funny videos that make fun of or discuss games, gaming communities, or the industry in general. They are typically shorter than five minutes.

- **Walkthrough:** These are how-to videos, normally a few minutes long, of a skilled gamer showing others how to accomplish some task in a video game.
- **Let's Play:** These videos, often fifteen minutes or longer, contain extensive gameplay footage. Garmendia and other YouTubers often make a Let's Play series of videos, in which they play an entire game over the course of several weeks.
- **Review:** These are independent reviews of video games. They are made to inform potential buyers about a game's strengths and weaknesses.

These are the main forms of videos found on gaming channels. While there are millions upon millions of gaming videos available on YouTube, they tend to all fit into these simple categories. Germán Garmendia is no exception to this.

From Hola to Juega

A new channel, JuegaGerman ("Play Germán"), was created in May 2013. Unlike HolaSoyGerman, which included a variety of different video formats, JuegaGerman is more strongly dedicated to video game content. Garmendia's style, however, remains consistent with his original videos. Just as on his original channel, he presents his videos with great enthusiasm and seemingly unending creativity.

There are a great deal of differences on JuegaGerman, however. With the staggering amount of video content available both on video game consoles as well as the internet itself, Garmendia and

Garmendia had a smooth transition into JuegaGerman, and his video game channel would soon launch him into the ranks of YouTube stardom.

Problems, Big and Small

Video games have become, for better or worse, linked to modern society. Some video games depict real-world events (the *Call of Duty* series, for example) and contain graphic violence or language. There are many ways in which video games can be deemed controversial, thus providing content for stars like Garmendia. One of the biggest issues related to video game YouTube content deals with broken or incomplete games. Many video games have their releases delayed due to technical glitches—or the company just releases them with the problems still present. This leads to gaming channels posting videos discussing what went wrong and what the company could have done to prevent the glitches. Sometimes, these videos are comical, poking fun at a small glitch, but they can also be harsh, demanding that a company fix its game.

Content creators, especially those of color, face other, more serious issues online, as well. In the video game world and beyond, many developers, executives, and gamers themselves have been accused of harassment, bullying, and other such things that sadly overshadow the release of new games or new videos. Female and racial minority gamers are often victims of online mobs, who join up to insult and harass their content and drive them offline. Though other parts of the internet face problems with harassment as well, video game communities can sometimes be closed off and not welcoming to others. This makes it difficult to find success for countless aspiring creators.

the many other gaming channels on YouTube can separate their videos based on the video games they are discussing. Additionally, Garmendia very frequently uploads vlogs to his channel. Vlogs are blogs shot on video that are commonly accompanied by text and other pieces of information and are a key feature used by

YouTubers of all varieties. Many famous YouTubers use vlogs as a key way to deliver content on their channels.

The Shapes of Vlogs

There are two main forms of vlogs found on YouTube: personal vlogs and live broadcasting vlogs. Personal vlogs are recorded by a single person and are mainly used to show off an event, vacation, or other fun or important subject. The audience for these forms of vlogs is commonly built-in subscribers who already follow the YouTube personality.

Vlogs are an essential part of many YouTube channels, including Garmendia's. They are easy to make and create an intimate relationship between creators and their audiences.

The other type of vlogs are live broadcasting (or livestreaming) blogs. In 2008, YouTube launched YouTube Live, a livestreaming feature. YouTube Live is often used by entertainment and corporate channels to announce product launches and other huge events for a wider audience. The main difference between these two types of vlogs is the amount of people the content reaches. Live broadcasting vlogs usually reach a wider audience, since they are produced by companies with bigger followings on YouTube. However, in some cases (including Garmendia's), a personal vlog may reach just as big of an audience. It all depends on the popularity of the channel presenting it.

Garmendia remains upbeat and charismatic despite the staggering amount of content he uploads to his gaming channel; he has even branched out into other fields, making him a multimedia celebrity.

One Busy Schedule

In addition to vlogging, one key difference between Garmendia's original channel and his new channel is the amount of content he produces on JuegaGerman. With his original channel, Garmendia was posting only a few times a week. Now, especially since he has established himself as a creator on YouTube, Garmendia sometimes uploads five or more videos per week to JuegaGerman.

Why so many posts? Are his viewers really this hungry for content? One would think he is in danger of burning himself out. However, his frequent uploads are related to the nature of gaming content itself. Because there are tens of millions of loyal video gamers out there, all hungry for content, Garmendia needs to keep posting to stay relevant. As with any internet celebrity, a fan base can disappear overnight if the content is not fresh, interesting, and frequent. If his channel does not fill the needs of his thirty million subscribers, someone else's will.

With the number of different games available to everyone today, Garmendia has various options and ways to reach a wider audience with his videos. If he wants, he can tailor his videos based on what games are increasing in popularity. If a game developer or company is in the news (whether it is for a good or bad reason), he can quickly create a vlog or parody video and let his followers know his own thoughts about the situation. This also speaks to the different ways video games are consumed in our society today. It is not enough to just review a game or discuss a difficult boss battle or specific level. Video games have become so important that every single aspect of them can be used as content on a YouTube site. Video games have become a huge part of mainstream culture, and Garmendia has a wide selection of ways to benefit from that popularity.

CHAPTER 3

The Growth of a Channel

Just looking at JuegaGerman's content confirms the staggering number of videos available on YouTube for people interested in video games. His channel is also proof that Garmendia knows how to use trends to his advantage. He is averaging a yearly upload schedule of more than two hundred videos. That speaks not only to the popularity of video gaming generally but to his own content more specifically. Thousands of games are released every year, so it is easy to see how Garmendia—and other gaming YouTubers— have plenty of options for content.

The Germán Playlist

Even among other YouTube stars, Garmendia is considered highly productive and organized. One look at his well-thought-out playlists confirms that reputation. He breaks down his videos according to the games he is reviewing, playing, or explaining, making it much easier for his followers to find the specific content they are looking for. This is a simple but effective method he uses for his channel. Rather than have a huge playlist of different videos, he categorizes them based on the specific content. If viewers, for example, are looking for a video about *Minecraft* or *Roblox*, they can simply look

Minecraft has made many appearances on Garmendia's channel; it is one of the most successful games of all time, popular among audiences of all ages.

to Garmendia's various playlists and find the specific content they are craving.

One example of Garmendia's well-organized playlists is that for the game *Sneak Thief*. *Sneak Thief* is a popular first-person shooter strategy game on the software service Steam, which allows its players to download a wide variety of games. In this game, the player explores different rooms, and the objective is to perform heists either by being as secretive as possible or by using absolute force as a means to break in and out.

Channels and Style

With countless games and even more videos, anyone interested in video games can use YouTube as a way to learn about the industry. There are multiple ways in which those with gaming channels, such as Garmendia, style their videos to entertain and educate their viewers. One is by simply reviewing the games themselves. Whether it is *FIFA*, *Call of Duty*, *The Elder Scrolls*, *Minecraft*, *Roblox*, or any of the thousands of other games available, a quick video review of the game (either recommending or disliking it) is one way those with gaming channels can reach an interested consumer.

Another style goes far beyond a simple review. What a lot of gaming stars, such as Garmendia, produce sometimes is called a Let's Play. These are much longer videos (sometimes exceeding an hour) that show a YouTube star going through and playing and exploring the game itself, showing viewers everything they would ever want to know about the game. This may seem too in-depth and complex, but it is a great way for newer players to learn more about the games they are playing and to seek help for certain parts of games that may be very challenging for them. Additionally, Let's Play videos have become extremely popular because they allow viewers to feel like they are gaming right alongside their favorite stars, enjoying their reactions and laughing right along with them.

It is easy to see how Garmendia has gained such a huge following through the way he plays *Sneak Thief*. One of the main barriers he has to overcome on his channels is the language barrier. He can speak English (as demonstrated in some of his videos). However, his primary language is Spanish. As he is playing, the commentary is all in Spanish. While it is possible to use a translation service to decipher what he is saying, one thing is clear, even to a viewer who cannot understand him: he is having fun.

The body language and mannerisms in all of Garmendia's videos are very clear to see. He is animated and engaged no matter what is happening. With the *Sneak Thief* videos as well as the others on the JuegaGerman channel, his passion and energy shine through. Whether he pulls off a successful heist in *Sneak Thief* or fails, he remains upbeat, enthusiastic, and entertaining. The main goal clearly is not necessarily to succeed with each mission as he plays.

More than simply winning, Garmendia is trying to show his users how these games can be entertaining and enjoyable. The object is not always to completely conquer a game. Rather, he is more focused on exploring hidden rooms, discovering secrets, and maximizing the gaming experience as a whole. His videos are a way for fans to watch and enjoy their favorite YouTuber having a good time.

Additional examples that demonstrate Garmendia's approach toward his gaming content are the videos he uploads to his *Roblox* playlist. *Roblox* is becoming a highly popular game to show on YouTube. One of the reasons behind its popularity is that the gaming experience is mainly designed by the players themselves. The *Roblox* community provides tools for its users to interact with other players as well as create their own games and worlds.

The Mighty, Mighty *Roblox*

In the mid-2010s, *Roblox* emerged as one of the most dominant gaming platforms online. There are many reasons for this. *Roblox* is more than a simple gaming site: it is a full-fledged online community. Players have unlimited resources at their disposal to create interactive games. Users play thousands upon thousands of customizable games with each other using *Roblox* as a guide. However, they are also encouraged to set up profiles, learn more about the other players they are online with, and establish friendships with their fellow gamers.

Roblox is not only a fun game for its users, it also serves as an interactive community, and users can befriend one another and create online relationships.

There are many popular games on *Roblox*, and Garmendia has taken notice and played many of them. For example, the game *MeepCity* has been played more than two billion times since it was created in February 2016. The beauty of *MeepCity* is that it is based in an enormous city, and there is not just one game that players like Garmendia can play. They can go go-karting, race each other throughout the online city, or just meet up and make new friends through the site itself. With features like this, it is easy to see why creators are able to produce regular content as well as maintain and add millions of subscribers.

Roblox also serves as a social media community. Social media sites such as Facebook, Twitter, YouTube, and Instagram allow users to share content and find people with similar interests who can become friends online. Roblox works in a similar way. Instead of sharing tweets, pictures, or statuses, however, online creators—along with notable celebrities, including Garmendia—can do something different with Roblox. They can create communities based on what games they are interested in or just explore a huge sprawling area like they do in MeepCity. Whatever their intentions are, online creators big (like Garmendia) and small (like his followers) can use the platform to make friends and explore new worlds and games together.

A New Channel, a New Start

JuegaGerman has millions of subscribers, and the world has recognized Garmendia as a legitimate digital influencer. Even his inactive HolaSoyGerman channel is the fourth-biggest channel on all of YouTube. JuegaGerman is the seventeenth-most-popular channel overall. His video game content has allowed him to translate his massive fan base into a community of video gaming followers. He has had an impact on the online gaming community as a whole, while also maintaining and building his own immense online audience. How did he do this with his video game content? Would it have made more sense for him to stick to his original channel instead, mixing in a video game review or walkthrough here and there?

Garmendia took a chance and launched his passion for video games into one of the most popular gaming channels on YouTube.

Even to non-Spanish-speaking viewers, his passion shines through. By focusing more heavily on video games, Garmendia is now able to focus his energies on making even more entertaining content. His followers know what to expect. While many may have initially been drawn to his channel for his original style, they can potentially find other creators that suit other needs while still following Garmendia for their gaming fix.

The separation between HolaSoyGerman and JuegaGerman is one of the more interesting aspects of the YouTube universe. The site truly lets both its creators and its subscribers discover and tap into their own interests. There also are countless creators for any interest one might have. Garmendia is far from the only online creator discussing the ins and outs of video games; there is an entire network of creators out there churning out content weekly. Garmendia, of course, just happens to be one of the biggest content creators in one of the most popular interest areas.

Chapter 4

Managing Success

Many YouTubers, including Logan Paul, shown here, have become controversial figures because of offensive or inappropriate content. Garmendia is always careful to stay away from poor behavior.

German Garmendia has used his massive online success in a very positive way. He refrains from overusing swear words and focuses instead on the games he loves. This is a very important unspoken rule he follows. Having one of the most popular gaming channels on YouTube comes with a responsibility that may not seem that obvious at first glance. Many YouTube celebrities become involved in controversies that may harm their status as creators or may cause them to lose fans. Whether it is related to the subject matter of their channels or not, it is important for YouTube sensations to realize that their every action is being monitored, and one slip-up can damage their careers.

Standing Guard

Creators such as Garmendia have used the internet to become true celebrities. Because everything they post is online—and anything posted online lasts forever—these creators must take special care to avoid posting harmful content. YouTube has policies established in order to curb harassment and cyberbullying. However, due to the staggering number of people who use YouTube every day, it is an unfortunate fact that these instances still occur and go unpunished for long periods of time.

This is where big-name stars come into play. By focusing on the games he enjoys, Garmendia is able to remain a positive influence for the YouTube community. He can even churn out content that makes fun of this negative side of YouTube. He has done this, with several videos condemning the idea of trolling. Trolling is when people on YouTube post hateful, hurtful messages and videos in order to purposely anger people online.

With millions of subscribers devoted to his posts, Garmendia—whether he means to or not—acts as a role model to reduce these negative behaviors. In this regard, he is not merely a goofy, charismatic lover of video games. He is defending the integrity of YouTube as a whole, ensuring that everyone can remain safe online without worrying about dealing with troll trouble. Like many creators, he has risen to the occasion by simply making sure that harassment and bullying do not become an ongoing issue. Their videos and positive attitudes can act as shields against online bullying and misbehavior.

Playing Well with Others

Collaboration videos, which are popular in both gaming communities and YouTube as a whole, are a big part of digital stardom. This means that instead of one person in a YouTube video, multiple content creators appear. This may be done for special game releases or for significant anniversaries or milestones (how long someone has been on YouTube, a new follower count, etc.). Countless videos are put together starring multiple online creators. While it may seem counterproductive for these creators to star in videos together, there is also obvious value to it. Stars like Garmendia can give opportunities to lesser-known YouTubers to establish themselves online and gain a following. The YouTube universe is so immense that there is room for more and more stars to emerge each and every day, and many are happy to work with one another to achieve even greater success.

Another way collaboration occurs on YouTube does not necessarily involve multiple independent creators. It often happens between a creator and a game company or developer. Many times, gaming companies will call upon stars, such as Garmendia, to boost sales for a specific game or to raise awareness for a game that may not be selling as well as the companies had hoped. This is exactly what happened in early 2018 when the gaming company FuturePlay called on Garmendia to help it with the game *Craft Away!* This game, similar to *Roblox*'s *MeepCity*, allows its users to interact in an enormous gaming atmosphere, playing minigames and enjoying specific adventures along the way.

Garmendia collaborated with FuturePlay on a marketing campaign designed to encourage more people to download *Craft Away!* Marketing campaigns are a planned series of events that are designed to promote an individual resource, product, or service. While FuturePlay and Garmendia were initially going to produce just one video to help launch the game, his video proved to be such a hit for its product that they wound up making several more videos together, showcasing the ins and outs of the game itself. The results of this were great news for FuturePlay. The company used Garmendia's influence to drive traffic and downloads toward its new

Garmendia has been able to use his channel to help promote and market games because he has such a wide platform. This helps the developers get their game out there and further builds Garmendia's channel.

title. FuturePlay knew what it was doing when it reached out to a young YouTuber to help spread the word about its new game.

This collaboration speaks to Garmendia's power as an influencer. Simply put, an influencer is someone who can help

31

61

4.807M   121

5.39K   282   763   2.51K

77   10   6   2   1

Level Up!   Level Up!   Level Up!   Level Up!
941K   943   3.87K   15.8K

With Garmendia's help, the mobile game *Craft Away!* gained thousands of users in a short time and proved that leveraging a YouTube star's fame can be beneficial to companies.

drive a product—such as *Craft Away!*—to staggering heights. Influencers come in all shapes and sizes. In Garmendia's case, it is easy to see why a gaming company would rely on him to play and help sell a game. Given his extreme popularity online, it is no wonder the game performed like it did. Enticed by Garmendia's passion and enthusiasm, FuturePlay used the relatively new platform of YouTube marketing to drive the growth of the product. There's no telling if *Craft Away!* would have been a success had it not been for Garmendia and his influence. However, there is no question that the online star helped the company out tremendously.

Spanish-Speaking Stardom

Garmendia has stated that he controls all the content on his channel. His background is one major contributor to his content and his success. Latin American countries are the base of Garmendia's success, but they are far from his only supporters. Still, his Spanish-speaking fan base makes up the core of his subscriber count, and everything he produces helps his popularity grow in that community.

Latin American countries look to YouTube for their entertainment more than they depend on regular television productions and channels. WhatsApp and similar messaging apps remain among the most downloaded smartphone applications in Latin American countries, but YouTube is often close behind. Many of these users rely on YouTube to get their daily dose of news, entertainment, and relaxation.

Another way to explain Garmendia's popularity in Spanish-speaking countries is through the world of telenovelas. Televenovelas are Spanish-language dramas that heavily use overdramatizing—something that Garmendia does consistently in his videos. By copying the kind of acting found in these beloved shows, he is representing a larger part of Latin American culture. Actors in telenovelas are commonly (and purposefully) overacting or overreacting in scenes they are in. Garmendia is the same way. A simple breakthrough in a video game he has been playing for a long time becomes something much more exaggerated. By acting like a beloved actor in a telenovela, Garmendia draws people to

Telenovelas and Soap Operas

Garmendia's style being similar to telenovelas makes logical sense, considering that telenovelas are a huge part of Spanish-speaking culture and he is from Chile, a Spanish-speaking country. Telenovelas are often confused with shows more familiar to American audiences: soap operas. They are quite similar, mainly in how overdramatized the action is. However, there are key differences.

Soap operas commonly air during daytime hours. Telenovelas, on the other hand, air both in the afternoon and during prime time, giving people several chances to watch the shows. Also, telenovela actors are regarded with great esteem and are usually the top tier of actors in Spanish-speaking countries. American soap opera performers are often seen as a lesser tier of actors. Both of these genres, however, rely on constant plot twists, backstabbing, and intense overacting. Regardless of the differences between them, both soap operas and telenovelas are beloved in their respective cultures.

A telenovela episode and a video from JuegaGerman will have many similarities; much of Garmendia's comedic sense is influenced by telenovelas.

himself and his antics in gaming videos because they see something familiar in him. They are used to the kind of acting he employs, and they really like it.

There is also a universal appeal in how Garmendia presents his videos. There is an authentic do-it-yourself style to every video he produces. It would be easy for him to fake interest in the video games he plays and reviews, but anyone who watches any of his videos can see this is not the case. He is constantly smiling, laughing, and showing genuine interest. His passion for whatever game he is currently playing shines through in each and every video he posts on JuegaGerman. Regardless of whether he has built his fan base through his connections to the telenovela style or his infectious energy, Garmendia has become an icon in the YouTube community.

More than a YouTuber

Germán Garmendia has undeniably made his mark in the world of YouTube. He is one of the most popular creators online, and there is no telling how far he'll go with the constant video gaming, comedy, and other content he produces. He is a pioneer of the online gaming community, but he wants more. He has already transferred his YouTube fame into other successful ventures. He has a best-selling book titled *#ChupaElPerro: Uno Que Otro Consejo: Para Que No Te Pase Lo Que a Un Amigo (#ChupaElPerro: A Little Advice So What Happened to Your Friend Doesn't Happen to You)*. Another Garmendia book, *Di Hola (Say Hello)*, was released in 2018. He has also broken into the world of movies, lending his voice to the Spanish-language adaptation of 2016's *Ice Age: Collision Course*. Not satisfied with that, he has also signed a sponsorship deal with Reebok and had LG sponsor one of his videos. He has won various YouTube awards, and with more than forty million subscribers between both his channels, his net worth is in the millions of dollars.

There is truly no telling how successful Garmendia will become. The era of YouTube celebrities is still young, and his content continues to draw in new subscribers every month. However, there is the issue of whether he can maintain and build on his success because his content is in Spanish. While many creators on YouTube—including Garmendia, El Rubius, and countless others— have found huge success as Spanish-speaking creators, that may not translate into worldwide fame on other platforms. Only time will tell, but it is clear that if Garmendia wants to stay on top, he will have to continue adapting and improving his content, just as he has done his entire career.

With an undeniable energy, a genuine love for the games he is playing, and a reliable, constant production of content, Garmendia has provided endless hours of content for his subscribers through JuegaGerman. He lays claim to two of the most popular channels on all of YouTube, each one unique. He is one of the countless examples of people on YouTube who have thrown themselves into their passion, making it a profitable career. It cannot be denied that Garmendia has made his mark on online gaming in the digital age. He truly cares about the games he plays and tries his best to foster a safe community online. It will be fascinating to see how the channel develops and how Garmendia will continue using video games to entertain and inspire his tens of millions of fans.

TIMELINE

April 1990 Germán Garmendia is born in Copiapó, Chile.

December 1993 Garmendia's father dies in a car accident.

2003 Garmendia forms a band called Zudex with his brother.

2011 Encouraged by his friends, Garmendia uploads his very first video to YouTube. He also starts his first channel, HolaSoyGerman.

2013 Garmendia begins uploading video game content to his channel JuegaGerman. He is accused of using bot websites to falsely pad his follower stats. He reaches one million subscribers in December.

2014 Garmendia wins the Icon of the Year prize from YouTube Rewind. He makes a brief appearance in YouTube Rewind 2014. He reaches five million subscribers in October.

November 2015 Garmendia reaches ten million subscribers on YouTube.

2016 Garmendia releases his book *#ChupaElPerro: Uno Que Otro Consejo: Para Que No Te Pase Lo Que a Un Amigo* in Latin America and Spain in April. He voices Julian in the Spanish version of *Ice Age: Collision Course*. He reaches fifteen million subscribers in September. He earns a spot on *Forbes*'s list of top-earning YouTubers, with an estimated worth of $5.5 million.

June 2017 Garmendia reaches twenty million subscribers on YouTube.

March 2018 Garmendia reaches twenty-five million subscribers on YouTube. He releases a new book, *Di Hola*.

GLOSSARY

announcement A video produced by a company to let viewers know about an upcoming game.

collaboration The act of two channels joining together to produce content on YouTube.

content Any video or music uploaded to a YouTube channel.

creator Someone who writes, records, produces, and publishes content online.

demo A short tutorial on how a video game is played.

followers Synonymous with "subscribers"; anyone who follows or engages with a channel.

gameplay The ins and outs of how a certain video game is played.

gamers Those interested in playing video games and watching video game content.

launch A video that reminds consumers that a game will soon be released or available.

Let's Play A video that is commonly longer and includes intensive gameplay of a particular game.

marketing campaign A planned set of activities used to promote a product or service.

review A video that praises or criticizes a particular video game.

Roblox A large online gaming community where users can interact, create worlds, and play games.

subscriber Someone who follows a channel and is notified when that channel uploads new content.

telenovela A genre of Spanish television known for plot twists and extreme overacting.

trolling Negative, harmful online behavior done on purpose to try to enrage and annoy others.

vlog A video blog published online.

AbleGamers Charity

PO Box 508

Charlestown, WV 25414

Website: https://ablegamers.org

Facebook and Twitter: @AbleGamersCharity

This charity offers video games as a way to engage the disabled community through digital means.

Entertainment Software Association

601 Massachusetts Avenue NW, Suite 300

Washington, DC 20001

Website: http://www.theesa.com

Facebook: @TheEntertainmentSoftwareAssociation

Twitter: @theESA

This association represents both video game creators and businesses, handling both production and public affairs concerns.

Entertainment Software Association of Canada (ESAC)

130 Spadina Avenue

Toronto, ON, Canada M5V 2L4

Website: http://www.theesa.ca

Facebook: @EntertainmentSoftwareAssociationCanada

Twitter: @EASCanada

The ESAC serves to ensure that Canada is a place where people can safely develop, play, and discuss video games.

Gamers Outreach

PO Box 695

Saline, MI 48176

Website: https://gamersoutreach.org

Facebook, Twitter, and Instagram: @GamersOutreach

This nonprofit uses video games as a way to help hospitalized children cope with treatment.

International Game Developers Association (IGDA)

150 Eglinton Avenue

Toronto, ON, Canada M4P 1E8

Website: https://www.igda.org

Facebook and Twitter: @IGDA

This nonprofit association offers support for video game creators around the world.

National Alliance on Mental Illness

3803 N. Fairfax Drive, Suite 100

Arlington, VA 22203

Website: https://www.nami.org

Facebook: @NAMI

Twitter and Instagram: @NAMICommunicate

This organization, based in the United States, helps educate people about and advocate for those with mental illnesses, including YouTube creators feeling the pressure of the digital world.

YouTube

901 Cherry Avenue

San Bruno, CA 94066

Website: http://www.youtube.com

Facebook and Twitter: @YouTube

YouTube offers countless videos on every imaginable topic,
including video games, and also hosts other forms of entertainment.

FOR FURTHER READING

Bay, Jason W. *Start Your Video Game Career: Proven Advice on Jobs, Education, Interviews, and More for Starting and Succeeding in the Video Game Industry*. Middletown, DE: Game Industry Career Guide, 2017.

Ciampa, Rob, et al. *YouTube Channels for Dummies*. Hoboken, NJ: John Wiley & Sons, 2015.

Garmendia, Germán. *#ChupaElPerro: Uno Que Otro Consejo: Para Que No Te Pase Lo Que a Un Amigo*. Madrid, Spain: Altea, 2016.

Graham, P. J. *Video Game Addiction*. San Diego, CA: ReferencePoint Press, 2019.

Hansen, Dustin. *Game On! Video Game History from* Pong *to* Pac-Man *to* Mario*,* Minecraft*, and More*. New York, NY: Fiewel & Friends, 2016.

McCarthy, Cecilia Pinto. *E-sports Game Design*. Chicago, IL: Norwood House Press, 2018.

Owen, Ruth. *The Wonderful Worlds of a Video Game Designer*. St. Austell, UK: Ruby Tuesday Books, 2016.

Polydoros, Lori, and Aaron Sautter. *Awesome Video Game Competitions*. Oxford, UK: Raintree, 2018.

Roesler, Jill. *Online Gaming: 12 Things You Need to Know*. Mankato, MN: 12-Story Library, 2016.

Scholastic. *Gaming Live! Your Guide to Video Game Livestreaming*. New York, NY: Scholastic, 2016.

BIBLIOGRAPHY

Condis, Megan. *Gaming Masculinity: Trolls, Fake Geeks & the Gendered Battle for Online Culture*. Iowa City, IA: University of Iowa Press, 2018.

Donovan, Sandra. *Technology Top Tens*. Minneapolis, MN: Lerner Publications, 2015.

Forbes. "Streaming Celebrities." Retrieved December 10, 2018. https://www.forbes.com/pictures/gjdm45ffed/streaming -celebrities/#7f21e664334c.

Matchmade. "Case Study: Launching *Craft Away!* with JuegaGerman and 25 Million Subscribers." September 14, 2018. http://matchmade.tv/studies/2018-01-31-juegagerman.

Pandell, Lexi. "Meet Germán Garmendia, the Aggressively Normal YouTube Superstar Who Wants It All." *Wired*, June 13, 2018. http://www.wired.com/story/meet-german-garmendia-the -aggressively-normal-youtube-superstar-who-wants-it-all.

Parkin, Simon. "The YouTube Stars Heading for Burnout: 'The Most Fun Job Imaginable Became Deeply Bleak.'" *Guardian*, September 8, 2018. http://www.theguardian.com /technology/2018/sep/08/youtube-stars-burnout-fun-bleak -stressed.

Popper, Ben. "2017 Was YouTube's Best Year Ever. It Was Also Its Worst." Verge, December 22, 2017. https://www.theverge .com/2017/12/22/16805410/youtube-business-scandals-best -worst-year

Wolf, Mark J. P. *Video Games FAQ: All That's Left to Know About Games and Gaming Culture*. Montclair, NJ: Backbeat Books, 2017.

INDEX

About the Author

Kevin Hall has written several books for Rosen Publishing, including one about how to create and maintain your own YouTube channel. He did rigorous research on YouTube to complete this book and has learned many valuable things about the website.

Photo Credits

Cover Victor Chavez/WireImage/Getty Images; p. 4 Piotr Swat/Shutterstock.com; p. 6 Luis Padilla/Photodisc/Getty Images; p. 8 De Visu/Shutterstock.com; p. 10 NurPhoto/Getty Images; p. 12 Bloomberg/Getty Images; p. 15 Miguel Larrauri/Newscom; p. 17 The Washington Post/Getty Images; p. 18 Ariel Ojeda/Newscom; p. 21 Mark Ralston/AFP/Getty Images; p. 24 Sharaf Maksumov/Shutterstock.com; p. 26 Frazer Harrison/Getty Images; p. 28 Todd Williamson/WireImage/Getty Images; p. 31 Frederick M. Brown/Getty Images; p. 32 Courtesy Futureplay Games; p. 34 National Geographic Image Collection/Alamy Stock Photo; cover, p. 1 triangle pattern Maxger/Shutterstock.com; cover vertical pattern chanchai howharn/Shutterstock.com; back cover pattern Onchira Wongsiri/Shutterstock.com; interior pages hexagon pattern Ink Drop/Shutterstock.com; interior pages additional geometric pattern Iuzvykova Iaroslava/Shutterstock.com.

Design/Layout: Brian Garvey; Editor: Siyavush Saidian; Photo Researcher: Nicole DiMella